ABUNDANT-LIFE GRACE

ABUNDANT-LIFE GRACE

*Experiencing the Gift
of a Satisfying Abundant Life*

Dennis G. Aaberg

XULON PRESS

Xulon Press
2301 Lucien Way #415
Maitland, FL 32751
407.339.4217
www.xulonpress.com

Xulon PRESS

© 2023 by Dennis G. Aaberg

All rights reserved solely by the author. The author guarantees all contents are original and do not infringe upon the legal rights of any other person or work. No part of this book may be reproduced in any form without the permission of the author.

Due to the changing nature of the Internet, if there are any web addresses, links, or URLs included in this manuscript, these may have been altered and may no longer be accessible. The views and opinions shared in this book belong solely to the author and do not necessarily reflect those of the publisher. The publisher therefore disclaims responsibility for the views or opinions expressed within the work.

Unless otherwise indicated, Scripture quotations taken from the Holy Bible, New Living Translation (NLT). Copyright ©1996, 2004, 2007 by Tyndale House Foundation. Used by permission of Tyndale House Publishers, Inc.

Scripture quotations taken from the King James Version (KJV) – *public domain*.

Note from author:

All Scripture quotations are italicized for emphasis and clarity.

When referring to God, the words He, Him, His are capitalized to show reverence; except in Bible quotes where lower case is maintained.

Paperback ISBN-13: 978-1-66287-714-8
Ebook ISBN-13: 978-1-66287-715-5

Table of Contents

Dedication xi
Introduction xiii

Chapter 1: GRACE INITIATED: Identifying and
Embracing the God in Your Life 1
- What You Can't Get Enough Of 1
- The Lifetime Search 2
- Explaining the Unexplainable 3
- Benefits of Christ-followers 4
- Decision-making Process 6
- Where Is Your Focus? 7
- Free-will: The Critical Choice 8
- The World We Live In 9
- Lessons from 9/11/2001 9
- Division of Church and State 10

Chapter 2: GRACE ACQUIRED: Growing Intimacy
with God and Self 13

- Why Are so Many Christians Not Experiencing
  Abundance? 13
- Forfeiting Blessings through Distorted Teaching 14
- Intimacy through Pain 15
- The Ultimate Goal of Painful Adversities 17

- Anger, Pain, and Fear 18
- Where Does Anger Come From? 20
- The Gift of Wisdom 21
- Testing Our Perceived Wisdom 23
- Wisdom for Life's Battles 25
- Godly versus Worldly Peace 26
- Our Limiting Enemy – Unbelief 28
- The Power to Obey: But Obey What? 29
- Ignoring the Source of Power 30
- Recognizing Truth 31

Chapter 3: LIVING THE GRACE-FILLED LIFE: Finishing Well 33

- Source of Sensitivity 35
- Knowing Yourself 36
- Fateful Requests 38
- Embracing Your Calling 40
- Separating Behavior from the Offender 41
- Grace versus Law 42
- The Greatness of God 43
- Inevitable Faith Tests 44
- What Makes Pursuits Right or Wrong? – Godly or Ungodly? 45
- Daily Life Choices 47
- Ungodly Influencers 48
- Let Peace Rule in Your Heart 49
- Believe – Forgive – Speak – Receive 51
- Work Required on Our Part 52
- Love and Freedom 54
- The Spirit that Overcomes Fear 55
- Walking in Truth: God's Requirements 56

- Sufferings of the Faithful........................ 58
- The One Joyful Suffering........................ 60
- Called into the Battle............................61
- World at War: Need for Godly Wisdom..........61
- Bottom Line 62
- Final Thoughts 63

Other Books by the Author 65

Dedication

I dedicate this book to my Lord and Savior, Christ Jesus, Who has truly endowed me with every good and perfect gift for my well-being in this life.

There is an old axiom that goes, "No pain, no gain." I have recognized in hindsight that every painful experience in my life has led me into a deeper understanding of God's love for me, and that has led to increasing intimacy with God.

So, as I continue to dedicate my life to seeking the LORD JESUS with all my heart, mind, soul, and strength and enjoy the many benefits and rewards in doing so, I pray you will do the same to experience all the goodness in God.

God bless you in your journey to intimacy with God in Christ Jesus, Who loved you enough to give His life in exchange for yours.

Introduction

If you consider the Bible simply a collection of books written by men about God from their own insights and perspectives and records of historical events, you will receive very little benefit from it.

The Bible is a living and breathing organism: God's revelation of Himself. In it, He reveals His character and love for His creation, and humankind is the crown jewel of His earthly creations. As we earnestly seek intimacy with God through prayer and His living and breathing revelation of Himself—the Holy Bible—we continually grow in our eagerness for more.

So, I invite you to realize that when you read your Bible, you are actually communing with the God of all creation and the Redeemer of your soul, Who desperately wants you to know Him intimately and experience His goodness, love, and compassion.

But, as in any relationship, you will only get out of it what you put into it and only receive what you expect from it. So, I encourage you to earnestly seek to grow your relationship with the One True Living God, Who loves you more than you can comprehend.

My hope is you too will come to a heart-felt knowledge of His love for you that will assist you in walking daily with an inner-peace and contentment that God seeks for all His children; a peace and contentment the unbelieving will never fully comprehend without surrendering their life to Jesus.

God bless!

Chapter 1:

GRACE INITIATED

Identifying and Embracing the God in Your Life

WHAT YOU CAN'T GET ENOUGH OF

In a recent men's Bible study, the comment was made, *"Whatever you can't get enough of is your God."* The comment came after my comment that *"I can't get enough of God, and those who love money can never get enough money."* Both thoughts were generated while studying the first chapter in the Book of James.

Having come to recognize God's constant, active presence in my life, I find myself increasingly wanting to know my God, Father, and Friend more intimately. Deeper revelations of His character and love for me and all of His creation come to me daily as I spend time in prayer and communing with Him in His Living Testimony—the Holy Bible. This is my desire for all humanity: to come to the realization of God's great love for us all and His desire to bless us beyond anything we can think or imagine based on our limited understanding of God's greatness.

Caution! Simply reading the Bible for information will likely not draw you closer to our LORD and Savior. Revelation from God requires an earnest heart-search to *know* Him and *seek* Him with *expectation*. We are encouraged to seek God with our entire being—heart, soul (mind, will, emotions), and strength. When seeking God with our entire being, *we can expect to receive every good thing* He has reserved for us—now and forevermore.

THE LIFETIME SEARCH

<u>Hebrews 11:6</u>
"And it is impossible to please God without faith. Anyone who wants to come to Him must believe that God exists and that He rewards those who sincerely seek Him."

God is the source of everything good and willing and eager to reward us as we dedicate ourselves to a lifetime of seeking intimacy with Him. He wants to be known! So, I ask again, who is your god? What or who are you diligently or sincerely seeking? What or who are you putting your trust in? Let's review some common gods to help ponder the answer to that question.

The Bible records the fact that if you love money, you will never acquire enough money to satisfy you. If focused on sexual pleasure, you will never have enough sex to satisfy you—you will always be left wanting and never satisfied. If you love power and control, you will never be satisfied either because no matter how powerful and controlling you become, there will always be someone with more power and control—God being the ultimate Sovereign, with unlimited power. Are you seeking to be most popular to boost your self-esteem? There will always be someone more popular to burst your bubble. Do you find your physical beauty the god that others worship to boost your pride and ego and, perhaps, use to manipulate others for your benefit? Even that physical beauty will fade with age. Are you seeking to boost your ego by being the toughest guy around? Once again, there will always be someone who is able to overpower you. No. The answer to a content life does not lie there.

When reviewing that brief list of worldly gods, do you see the underlying root? Pride! The pride of Satan woven into our nature through man's rebellion against God is our daily battle. That false god, pride, is ultimately at the root of every human evil and the demon we must all deal with and overcome through the power of the Spirit of Truth within us as believers in Christ Jesus. If we walk humbly with God and man, instead of competing for advantage with each other, the spirit of pride will lose its power to influence us.

EXPLAINING THE UNEXPLAINABLE

PRIDE! Not a single person is, or ever has been, fully delivered from the struggle with the desire to control life.

One of the symptoms of this struggle is our need to have an explanation for everything. But *if we could explain everything, we would be God*. We are not. There is only One God. Do you see the subtlety of pride? Think about it. Don't we tend to seek to understand and control all the conditions in our lives for our comfort and well-being or the comfort and well-being of our families? Don't we have a tendency to take offense at actions of others that are contrary to our expectations and many times want to control their actions to accommodate our comfort level? We ignorantly share our opinions on life believing we have all the solutions to the world's problems, when, in reality, we have very little understanding of how to run the world or the human race or even our own lives for that matter. Through our ignorance and pride, we tend to ruminate about all the perceived evil in the world and the actions of those who don't meet our expectations. How many times have you said, "*If I were God, I would* [you fill in the blank]."

And in our ignorance and need to know and have an answer for every unknown, we make up answers for unanswerable questions to make ourselves feel safe and comfortable in our unique corner of life. If we can formulate answers to questions only God has the answers for, it leaves us feeling a certain amount of imagined control and safety.

It takes a humble heart to admit we know very little and put our trust in a God we can't see or touch. But, if we can humble ourselves to surrender our well-being into the hands of God and trust Him to care for us, we will finally experience the peace and contentment we fail to find or achieve through our own efforts. Lasting inner-peace and contentment come only when we bring ourselves to that realization and submission.

BENEFITS OF CHRIST-FOLLOWERS

Experiencing the best possible life is found in developing intimacy with the God who created all things and knows each of us better than we will ever know ourselves because He designed each of us unique. We will experience our ultimate life experience by seeking Jesus for the best path for our lives. I would suggest taking a few minutes to reflect on the following passage from the book of Psalms, then offering it up as your prayer so you can move in the direction of your ultimate life experience.

Psalm 25:4-6
"Show me the right path, O LORD; point out the road for me to follow. Lead me by your truth and teach me, for you are the God who saves me."

The Psalms are loaded with God's promises of good for His children, which are all those who have accepted Christ as their Lord and Savior and Redeemer. Psalm 103 especially contains a substantial list of benefits that alone should entice any unbeliever to consider surrendering their life to Christ Jesus.

One of the tangible benefits of keeping our focus on God and relentlessly seeking Him through prayer and reading the Bible daily is an inner-peace and content tranquility ruling in our hearts, regardless of life's circumstances. This is truly a gift through faith that the world of unbelievers will never comprehend because it is only available to God's children.

Isaiah 26:3
"You will keep in perfect peace all who trust in you, all whose thoughts are fixed on you!"

John 6:63
"The Spirit alone gives eternal life. Human effort accomplishes nothing. And the very words I have spoken to you are spirit and life."

Eternal life, which begins the moment we accept Christ Jesus as LORD and Savior, is the ultimate benefit of believing in His life-giving sacrifice to pay our sin-debt and set us free from the power of sin (imperfection). And, as Jesus revealed, His very words are *spirit and life*, so when we saturate our heart and mind with His written words recorded in the Holy Bible, we receive spiritual and life-sustaining nourishment. That is why seeking God through daily Bible reading and study is so important.

John 5:24
"I tell you the truth, those who listen to my message and believe in God who sent me have eternal life. They will never be condemned for their sins, but they have already passed from death into life."

We also benefit from fellowshipping with other believers as we encourage and sharpen each other in spiritual matters and earthly living matters. We are not just spiritual beings. We have bodies made from the earth's elements that need physical care. Some in the body of Christ seem to ignore that reality and try making everything spiritual. That is a life-limiting mistake.

DECISION-MAKING PROCESS

Every action starts with a thought. Tens-of-thousands of thoughts (words/images) pass through our minds daily. Our challenge is to recognize which words and images come from the Living and True God and which ones come from the Enemy of our soul – Satan. We all face this choice—listen to God or listen to Satan. Some may argue, as we see in the Book of James, that our own desires entice us into sin (unhealthy choices), which is true, but that is, in essence, the same as choosing to listen to Satan. If our bodily senses lead us astray and we decide to surrender to the *lust of the flesh, the lust of the eyes, or the pride of life*, as recorded in 1 John 2:16, we surrender to the world's temptations. And the Bible clearly reveals, the world system is ruled by Satan.

2 Timothy 2:24-26 (emphasis added)
"A servant of the LORD must not quarrel but must be kind to everyone, be able to teach, and be patient with difficult people. **Gently instruct those who oppose the truth.** *Perhaps God will change those people's hearts and they will learn the truth. Then they will come to their senses and escape from the devil's trap.* **For they have been held captive by him to do whatever he wants.**"

So, we again face the reality that we will serve either God or Satan. Those are the only two choices available to us.

WHERE IS YOUR FOCUS?

Knowing that none of us can escape the uncertainties and unknowns in life, and recognizing that nearly all national media outlets are focused on feeding us fear-based messages twenty-four hours a day, where are you going to focus your attention? Will you focus on fear-generated messages of the world or faith-generated messages from Jesus—the God of mercy, truth, compassion, and grace? Will you choose to believe His promises to protect and prosper those who accept Him as LORD and Savior and walk humbly with Him?

I have become fully convinced that God's promises are most certainly true. But, for His promises to benefit you, you must first recognize your need for God; surrender your will into His hands by accepting Christ Jesus as your Savior, and then spend your life diligently seeking Him for truth, wisdom, understanding, and knowledge of His great love for you and then rest in His promises instead of the fear-based messages propagated daily.

Diligently seeking God daily results in restored souls and an ever-increasing ability to face the trials of life with inner-peace and contentment, knowing God is with you every step of the way and, in fact, directing your steps down the best path for your life. You will never comprehend fully the ways of God, but as you seek Him for wisdom and understanding daily, He releases increasing wisdom and understanding to you. As you grow in intimacy with Him, you will slowly over time come to love and appreciate Him more, and that will drive you to want more and more of Him.

FREE-WILL: THE CRITICAL CHOICE

Free-will is a controversial topic within Christian churches, as well as society itself. What does free-will really mean?

I have come to believe, based on my current understanding of God's revelation to me, our free-will involves making one of two choices. We are born with free-will to surrender our will into the hands of God to direct or to rebel against God's design for us, choosing instead to allow Satan to direct our path through self-centeredness and pride.

The Bible makes it abundantly clear God has a preferred perfect path for our lives. If we recognize our dependence on God, accept Him as LORD and Savior, and surrender our hearts to Him to direct, we will embrace His design for our life and flow in His Spirit's direction. He promises to guide our steps down the best path for our life, protect us along that path, and provide every good thing for our well-being as we confidently walk it. Choosing to rebel against God's design for our life is evidenced through mental and emotional pain and torment, constant anxiety and dissatisfaction with life, constantly comparing our life situations to others, and ultimately living miserable lives that end in fear and discouragement.

THE WORLD WE LIVE IN

We live in a very selfish and narcissistic world; a predominantly humanistic world that believes human wisdom (worldly wisdom) is sufficient to solve all human and earthly problems without involving God. Searching historical records, especially the Bible, reveals this cycle repeated countless times. In searching for truth, we recognize that this cycle of rejecting God in preference to self never ends well. Rebelling against God's design-plan has always resulted in collapsed societies and kingdoms. The collapse either drives the survivors back to God or into suicidal hopelessness when failing to recognize their need for God and His outstretched arms to receive them.

Sadly, we see this cycle repeat time after time. God rescues the repentant who cry out to Him, prospers them as they put their trust in Him, then let's them self-destruct when they become prosperous and start thinking they did it on their own and reject Him again. Then, when society hits bottom again and cries out to God for help, He again intervenes through His compassion and love to lift us up and prosper us once again. Why does history continue to repeat itself? Because of stubborn, prideful, rebellious hearts focused on self-will instead of God's will.

LESSONS FROM 9/11/2001

The cycle I just referred to clearly played out in the tragedy of 9/11. Leading up to that tragic event, this nation was systematically seeking to remove the name of God and Jesus from our language and beginning to associate the Bible with hate-speech. The halls of Congress, and even the Supreme Court, were joining forces to make humanism the religion of the land.

Then 9/11 happened, and we saw "God Bless America" signs and banners posted across our nation, and the very political leaders who were systematically working to eliminate the name of God and Jesus from our language were standing on the steps of the nation's capital, praying in concert for God's help. We saw prayer vigils on the steps of state capitals around the nation. But when things settled down and things began returning to normal after our Armed Forces eliminated some of the terrorist threats, it again became business as usual—we don't need God anymore.

So, the cycle came out of a reprieve and back to prideful business as usual. Our leaders built a Tower of Babel to replace the Twin Towers to demonstrate the pride of a nation. Basically, saying, *"No one will stop us! You cannot defeat us!"* Ignorantly believing it was by our own power we prevailed against a more evil enemy. I don't believe it is any coincidence we have seen increased natural disasters since that tragic period and lawlessness increasing. Any nation who rejects Christ Jesus will see increased lawlessness as God simply lifts His hand of protection and allows us to choose our own way over His and experience the consequences that go with that choice.

DIVISION OF CHURCH AND STATE

In Old Testament times, there was no division of church and state. There were many times when ungodly kings rebelled against God and His prophets and priests and suffered the consequences of destruction by sword, famine, and pestilence. But, they still consulted God through the prophets, even though they didn't always listen and obey. And time and again, they would reach the point of utter destruction, causing them to call out to God to save them again. God would take pity on them and rise up godly leaders to deliver them. God would again prosper them and protect them when they humbled themselves to once again live rooted in love, fairness, justice, and righteousness. The nations who sought God for direction always prospered, and God does not change. Nations seeking God for direction and choosing to listen to His direction will enjoy peace and provision.

There is no fence-sitting with God. We must choose: God or Satan; blessings or curses; abundant life or self-defeating life. The choice should be obvious, but the majorities are predicted (prophesied) to reject the ultimate offer of good and well-being found in Christ Jesus.

Chapter 2:

GRACE ACQUIRED

Growing Intimacy with God and Self

WHY ARE SO MANY CHRISTIANS NOT EXPERIENCING ABUNDANCE?

John 10:9-11 (KJV) (emphasis added)
"I am the door: by me if any man enter in, he shall be saved, and shall go in and out, and find pasture. The thief cometh not, but for to steal, and to kill, and to destroy: **I am come that they might have life, and that thy might have it more abundantly.** I am the good shepherd: the good shepherd giveth his life for the sheep."

A more modern translation might make even clearer what Jesus came to give us.

John 10:9-11 (NLT: emphasis added)
"Yes, I am the gate. Those who come in through me will be saved. They will come and go freely and will find good pastures. The thief's purpose is to steal and kill and destroy. **My purpose is to**

give them a rich and satisfying life. I am the good shepherd. The good shepherd sacrifices his life for the sheep."

Many Christians are not experiencing the freedom and abundant life Christ died to purchase for us. Why?

Many, if not most, Christians I come in contact with are still basically living under the *old covenant*, trying to please God by obeying a bunch of rules created through the distorted religious traditions of men or feverishly performing good deeds in an effort to pay God back. Even though Christian churches are rooted in the truth that Christ died for our sins, to pay our sin-debt once and for all, many still spend their lives afraid of incurring God's wrath for any missteps they might make or falling out of favor with God. I've been there and can relate. This is what we are taught from our youth, and it is the way of the world—love and favor are won or lost through personal performance. **Legalism kills the spirit of a believer and steals the abundant inner and external life Christ died to give us.**

FORFEITING BLESSINGS THROUGH DISTORTED TEACHING

One error I have encountered in Christian circles is the perverted teaching that says you have to live poor, or at least meagerly and miserly, to be a *good Christian*. The doctrine propagated through many Christian circles emphasizing false humility by denying themselves blessings in this life that God wants them to enjoy is really rooted in self-righteous pride. There is a lot of jealous and self-righteous finger-pointing in that crowd. False humility through sacrificing the good things

God offers us is probably one of the most common forms of self-deceptive pride within the body of Christ.

Here is a question for you: Why would God, the Creator of all things and Father to us as His believing children, deny us any good thing that would enhance our well-being? If we are grateful, obedient (loving) children, why would a good Father punish us by not fulfilling the good desires He has placed in our hearts? God spent thousands of years proving we cannot earn His favor through following rules. He is after our hearts! No one, other than Christ—God Himself in the flesh—has been able to obey *the Law* perfectly, so why do so many Christians still believe they are expected to live perfect lives to please God? Perversion of the gospel! Men over time have perverted the Good News for their own purposes, and *we sheep* have, for the most part, believed the distorted views of God's will for us.

INTIMACY THROUGH PAIN

There is an old axiom relating to building bodily muscles: "No pain, no gain." The same applies to intimacy (close knowing) with God and all other relationships in life.

Even though I would like to avoid all pain and conflict, as I am sure most would, it seems our mental and emotional health tend to predominantly grow through painful adversity and temptations. Adversity and temptations come to test our faith. We are told these pains and adversities do not come from God, but they will most certainly come to each of us to test our faith and reveal our character and the state of our heart.

James 1:13-15
"And remember, when you are being tempted, do not say, 'God is tempting me.' God is never tempted to do wrong, and he never tempts anyone else. Temptation comes from our own desires, which entice us and drag us away. These desires give birth to sinful actions. And when sin is allowed to grow, it gives birth to death."

So, we see the five senses God gave us to thoroughly enjoy life and warn us of danger—sight, smell, taste, touch, and hearing—can cause us to crave ungodly fulfillment and lead us to destructive and unhealthy choices. But, we do have another source of adversity and temptation.

1 Peter 5:7-9
"Give all your worries and cares to God, for he cares about you. Stay alert! Watch out for your great enemy, the devil. He prowls around like a roaring lion, looking for someone to devour. Stand firm against him, and be strong in your faith. Remember that your Christian brothers and sisters all over the world are going through the same kind of suffering you are."

We have a real spiritual enemy, who primarily works in our minds to accomplish his evil. He is identified by various names: Satan, Lucifer, Devil, Slanderer, and others. He is a formidable enemy.

THE ULTIMATE GOAL OF PAINFUL ADVERSITIES

If adversity and temptations are inevitable and necessary for our mental, spiritual, and emotional healthy growth, we need understanding and wisdom concerning them.

1 Peter 1:6-7
"So be truly glad. There is wonderful joy ahead, even though you have to endure many trials for a little while. These trials will show that your faith is genuine. It is being tested as fire tests and purifies gold – though your faith is far more precious than mere gold. So when your faith remains strong through many trials, it will bring you much praise and glory and honor on the day when Jesus Christ is revealed to the whole world."

James 1:2-4
"Dear brothers and sisters, when troubles come your way, consider it an opportunity for great joy. For you know that when your faith is tested, your endurance has a chance to grow. So let it grow, for when your endurance is fully developed, you will be perfect (mature) and complete, needing nothing."

So, we see trials and temptations have the same effect on our soul as weightlifting has on our physical body; both are designed to grow our strength. Just as our physical bodies need nourishment and resistance exercise to grow healthy and strong, our souls need nourishment from the Word of God and faith-tests to strengthen them. Just as our body systems and muscles atrophy and waste away without proper nutrition and exercise, our souls will atrophy and waste away without proper nutrition and exercise.

ANGER, PAIN, AND FEAR

I dare say, the vast majority of the human race blames someone other than themselves for the emotional pain they experience. Certainly, people do and say things that we might take offense to, and *taking* that offense can cause anger, resentment, and bitterness within us—but why?

I have never enjoyed pain, especially emotional pain, but physical pain has been a near constant companion throughout my life. I have been physically active all my life and played organized sports for forty consecutive years. Throughout my life of activity and sports, I have endured many physical injuries and pains. To me, the physical pains have been acceptable because I incurred them living the active life God designed for me—a life that has brought me much pleasure and fulfillment—especially through passing on skills to youth through coaching and being a godly influence in their lives. I wouldn't trade my active life for a safer, pain-free life for anything. So, in spite of the many residual pains from injuries that I still live with, I continue to enjoy living an active life and ignoring the pain as much as possible.

For me, emotional pain strikes deeper, but God has been there for me every step of the way and has not wasted a single pain. Through the emotional pains in my life, Christ Jesus has proven His faithfulness toward me and grown our intimacy as I increasingly come to recognize and appreciate His love for me and His constant caring, active presence. The words recorded in Romans 8:28 summarize beautifully the truth I have experienced over time as God continues to reveal a deeper understanding of His love for me:

Romans 8:28
"And we know that God causes everything to work together for the good of those who love God and are called according to His purpose for them."

I have lived long enough to experience the truth of that statement for myself. Along the way, I have experienced emotional pains I would not wish on anyone, but now, in hindsight, I wouldn't trade any of those painful experiences because God has used them all to benefit me in some way and, in return, enabled me to relate to and comfort others in their pain. Even though God did not author the painful events, He most certainly was in the midst of those battles with me, providing strength, comfort, and deliverance. And, on the other side of the victory, I experienced the rewards of increased wisdom, understanding, and strength to face the next battle. I have never believed in coincidence or luck. There is a design to the seeming madness and uncertainties in life.

Ecclesiastes 10:14 + 11:5 excerpt
"(10:14) No one really knows that is going to happen; no one can predict the future. (11:5) Just as you cannot understand the path of the wind or the mystery of a tiny baby growing in its mother's womb, so you cannot understand the activity of God, who does all things."

WHERE DOES ANGER COME FROM?

Anger is always generated from one of two sources: self-concern or injustice.

The more I have reflected on those truths, the more I've seen the truth of it in my own life. Today, while reflecting on my life, I recalled many happy memories. In the midst of reminiscing, the thought came that whenever I was angry, frustrated, or having a pity-party, it was because things were not going the way I thought they should or the way I wanted them to. Frustrated expectations (disappointments) had occurred. It was nearly always rooted in self-concern, fretting over what could go wrong or unmet expectations from myself or others. I might add, my biggest disappointments have been in myself for failing to meet unreasonable expectations I unconsciously set for myself; but also, for expecting others to meet certain expectations I felt were reasonable to expect. Foolishness! Here is the kicker. As I sit here writing this, the thought came to me that many of those unreasonable expectations were seeds planted in my mind and heart by others throughout my life. I have no reason to believe you have not been affected similarly, living life according to pre-programmed beliefs and life-directions others have infused that are not core to your God-design.

But there are times when anger is generated from witnessing evil and injustices. Jesus demonstrated *righteous anger* in the Temple when He angrily drove out ungodly merchandizers and when He angrily confronted self-righteous religious leaders. So, anger in and of itself is not sin (wrong). The root cause of our anger is what we must understand when that emotion arises in us.

Therefore, I have come to believe all anger over not getting our way or people not meeting our expectations for our comfort level is certainly *unrighteous anger*. Our angry reactions in those situations nearly always produce division and resentment and bitterness. The only anger I can conceive as being righteous is the anger generated by witnessing injustices that violate God's character and common decency that is inherently known to all. In those instances, the anger, I believe, is a God-given reaction to evil and designed to prompt us into action to overcome or eliminate that evil.

There are circles of belief today that deny the reality of evil. They believe it to be just an illusion and all mentally generated. They deny we have a supernatural spiritual enemy seeking to devour our souls. They live on very dangerous ground because unless we have allowed ignorance to go to seed, we cannot deny evil exits in this world, and it will continue to devour as many souls as possible unless we stand firmly against it. So, we must constantly seek God for truth and understanding concerning our reactions to life events and circumstances.

THE GIFT OF WISDOM

The wise King Solomon said he sought the world over for wisdom, but it was not to be found. He always came back around to the realization that God is the only source of wisdom. True wisdom is not found in the world. Wisdom is found only in God, and He reveals wisdom to us through His recorded testimony—the Holy Bible—and through writers, pastors, teachers, and mature Christians, to whom He gives insights to explain His Word in a variety of ways to make it more understandable and expansive.

True wisdom is a gift from God, and we receive godly wisdom by sincerely asking Him for it. And as we seek, He increases our wisdom and understanding in several ways. He speaks truths directly to our heart through His Holy Spirit of Truth, leads us to specific books for insights and healing, brings the right person at the right time into our lives for our well-being, plants us in a body of believers where we can grow and serve optimally, and etcetera. God finds a multitude of ways to provide everything we need for our well-being and to grow in intimacy with Him.

<u>James 1:5-8</u>
"If you need wisdom, ask our generous God, and he will give it to you. He will not rebuke you for asking. But when you ask him, be sure that your faith is in God alone. Do not waver, for a person with divided loyalty is as unsettled as a wave of the sea that is blown and tossed by the wind. Such people should not expect to receive anything from the Lord. Their loyalty is divided between God and the world, and they are unstable in everything they do."

When James warns us not to waver when asking God for wisdom, I don't believe he is referring to doubts that may arise in our minds. He is clearly stating we cannot waver between believing godly wisdom and worldly wisdom. A wavering person would tend to believe the wisdom that suits their current selfish desires. If godly wisdom leads to a desired self-concerned outcome, they will follow that. If worldly wisdom leads to their desired self-concerned outcome, they will follow that. So, basically, a wavering person is not seeking God's will but only looking for the easiest path to instant relief or gratification.

This brings us back to right motives. God told the prophet Samuel that He looks at our hearts and knows our inner thoughts and character. *Our motives and inward intentions are huge in*

God's eyes. We can do right things for wrong, selfish motives. We can sometimes do wrong things with right heart motives. We cannot purely judge a person's heart by their actions because only God knows a person's heart. I would argue that we don't always know our own hearts because we can, at times, even deceive ourselves. Thank God, He knows us completely and finds ways to keep us on the path created for us, even though we may take some temporary detours along the way.

TESTING OUR PERCEIVED WISDOM

James 3:13-18 (emphasis added)
"If you are wise and understand God's ways, prove it by living an honorable life, doing good works with the humility that comes from wisdom. But if you are bitterly jealous and there is selfish ambition in your heart, don't cover up the truth with boasting and lying. **For jealousy and selfishness are not God's kind of wisdom. Such things are earthly, unspiritual, and demonic. For wherever there is jealousy and selfish ambition, there you will find disorder and evil of every kind. But the wisdom from above is first of all pure. It is also peace loving, gentle at all times, and willing to yield to others. It is full of mercy and good deeds. It shows no favoritism and is always sincere.** *And those who are peacemakers will plant seeds of peace and reap a harvest of righteousness."*

When earnestly seeking God's wisdom and direction, He will most certainly fulfill our request. The answer to any particular request may not be a welcome one—it may involve more effort or a direction we were not planning on or hoping for. But, if the direction is from God, He will give us the inner-peace and confidence to step out in the direction He gives us if we are truly seeking to do His perfect will and willing to, at times, do the hard but right thing instead of shirking our responsibility to take the easy way out.

Wisdom involves obedience (love), and love is seldom, if ever, effortless, but it should not feel like a heavy burden. To love God, love ourselves, and love others requires a heart-felt effort. But, that heart-felt effort will never feel like a burden if it is initiated by God. God provides the inner-peace, confidence, and strength to do anything He directs us to do. Anything we choose to do that feels like a burden must be questioned.

Matthew 11:28-30
"Then Jesus said, 'Come to me, all you who are weary and carry heavy burdens, and I will give you rest. Take my yoke upon you. Let me teach you, because I am humble and gentle at heart, and you will find rest for your souls. For my yoke is easy to bear, and the burden I give you is light.'"

Jesus sacrificed His life so we could enjoy a life of abundance and rest for our souls. Jesus did not come to make life more difficult—He came to set us free from mental and emotional oppression and from religious legalistic traditions of men that burden our soul. Jesus set us free to be who He created us to be, and He is the only One who can reveal our true identity and purpose to us, so *listen closely to that inner voice that resonates with your heart and soul.* As you diligently seek to know Jesus better, you will experience your cares melting away into godly confidence over time until you reach *"perfect and entire wanting nothing"* as the apostle James wrote.

Grace Acquired

WISDOM FOR LIFE'S BATTLES

The apostle Peter further helps us understand what growing in intimacy with God and man looks like.

<u>2 Peter 4-10 (emphasis added)</u>
"And because of his glory and excellence, he has given us great and precious promises. These are the promises that enable you to share his divine nature and escape the worlds' corruption caused by human desires. In view of all this, make every effort to respond to God's promises. ***Supplement your faith with a generous provision of moral excellence, and moral excellence with knowledge, and knowledge with self-control, and self-control with patient endurance, and patient endurance with godliness, and godliness with brotherly affection, and brotherly affection with love for everyone. The more you grow like this, the more productive and useful you will be in your knowledge of our Lord Jesus Christ.*** *But those who fail to develop in this way are shortsighted or blind, forgetting that they have been cleansed from their old sins."*

Knowing God intimately leads to receiving every good and perfect gift as we mature in grace and truth. God continues to unveil His character and love to us little-by-little as we seek a closer relationship with Him. As we talk (pray) to Him as our Best Friend, He works in our body, soul, and spirit to anchor us in unspeakable inner-peace and contentment that will cause the world of unbelievers to marvel at our hope and, hopefully, want it for themselves.

GODLY VERSUS WORLDLY PEACE

A supernatural inner-peace is gifted to those who acknowledge their need and desire for God through Christ Jesus. Supernatural peace of heart and soul, regardless of our circumstances, *is a gift of God*. This freedom was purchased with the blood of Jesus when He exchanged His life for ours, making believers righteous in the sight of God forever. The power to resist sinful and foolish temptations and overcome every adversity with calm assurance is available only through the indwelling Holy Spirit.

Then we have temporary world peace. The world has been at war since man's first rebellion against God, and there will always be someone who wants to take over the world, or a small portion of it, to satisfy their longing for more personal advantage or simply to feed their ego and pride. So, in this world, we will continue to experience conflicts arising and the battle between good and evil continuing. To actually believe perpetual world peace is possible without every human being surrendering their will to God is beyond ignorant hopefulness. But, inner-peace is achievable. It only requires our receiving it with faith and thanksgiving.

John 14:27 (Jesus speaking)
"I am leaving you with a gift – peace of mind and heart. And the peace I give is a gift the world cannot give. So don't be troubled or afraid."

John 14:15-18 (Jesus speaking)
"If you love me, obey my commandments. And I will ask the Father, and he will give you another Advocate, who will never leave you.

He is the Holy Spirit, who leads into all truth. The world cannot receive him, because it isn't looking for him and doesn't recognize him. But you know him, because he lives with you now and later will be in you. No, I will not abandon you as orphans. I will come to you."

In His upper room discourse on the night of His betrayal, Jesus told His disciples He was giving them *a new commandment: to love one another as He loved them.* This *new commandment*, I believe, is only possible through the power of the in-dwelling Holy Spirit. When Jesus referred to *the Law*, He referred to the Ten Commandments, and those Ten Commandments all revolve around the relationship between God and man and between man and man. They embody the love of God, as revealed clearly in the Book of Micah.

<u>Micah 6:8</u>
"No, O people, the LORD has told you what is good, and this is what he requires of you: to do what is right, to love mercy, and to walk humbly with your God."

We are told the law is made for the lawless, to keep order and control in society. For believers under the influence of the Holy Spirit, our desire is always to do the right thing, and the Holy Spirit gently convicts us of wrongdoing and gives us the power to repent of unhealthy choices if we get sidetracked. Therefore, we are no longer, as believers, needful of rules and regulations to control our behavior as we come to seek the Holy Spirit for truth. The caveat, however, is that we must be taught about God and teach our children about God through His written Word, the Holy Bible, to clearly discern His Spirit's voice from the world's voice. This growth in knowledge of God's love and His design for our lives comes through hearing God's Word preached in church and taught in Sunday school classes, daily seeking God's wisdom and direction through personal Bible study and prayer, and fellowshipping with mature believers. We will not grow sufficiently in God's wisdom, understanding, and knowledge in isolation.

OUR LIMITING ENEMY – UNBELIEF

<u>John 16:9</u>
"The world's sin is that it refuses to believe in me."

When Jesus visited His hometown, Nazareth, during His earthly ministry, He could perform very few miracles and heal very few sick because of their unbelief. There is a notable correlation between faith and receiving the good things of God. Do you pray with wishful thinking, knowing intellectually that God is able to answer your prayer, or do you pray from a heart-anchored faith that expects an answer from God based on His promise to give you whatever you ask for in His name, Jesus, that aligns with His will?

Have you been religiously and denominationally brainwashed into believing miracles no longer happen? That the power to raise the dead, unstop the ears of the deaf, heal the sick and lame, and cast out demons ended with the first century Church, or have you experienced the active presence of God today, as I have, still working through believers to work the same works the first century apostles and disciples worked through the authority given them in the name of Jesus and gifting of the Holy Spirit?

THE POWER TO OBEY: BUT OBEY WHAT?

Christ, who said, *"All things are possible for God,"* also said, *"All things are possible for those who believe."* So, I must ask, what do you believe? Do you believe you can do all things through Christ Who strengthens you? Are you living in divine health with the full assurance that Christ's sacrifice purchased your physical wholeness? Are your decisions driven more by fear (which is a demonic spirit) or based on your faith in God's promises? Do you even know God's promises that apply to you?

During His upper room discourse, Jesus emphasized what I call *the core of Christian theology*. I provide a comprehensive break-down of His instructions in the book *Jesus' Last Seminar – Preaching Love and Unity*, published in 2009 through Xulon Press. But for our purposes here, I want to emphasis the main point Jesus was driving home to His followers: *that they stay connected to Him and obey His new commandment to love one another unconditionally as He loves.* In John 14:15, we find Jesus saying, *"If you love me, obey my commandments."* Whenever Jesus or the apostles referred to the Law or commandments, they were referring to the Ten Commandments. **The Ten Commandments are about living in perfect harmony with God and man.**

As with any law or commandment, they can be viewed from a negative or a positive perspective. Many people view the Ten Commandments as a list of rules to obey that bring punishment for disobedience, which leads to seeing God as a merciless law-enforcer. I see them as a guide from a loving God to show us how to live in perfect harmony with God and mankind.

Obedience relates to submitting to the authority of another. I would prefer to think of obedience as love. Jesus said we would submit to His authority if we love Him. So, we obey the entirety of God's law by simply loving God and others by being sensitive to the needs of others and providing for their well-being when able and led by the Spirit to do so. This also applies to us.

The summation of Old Testament Law—the Ten Commandments—is to *love God with our entire being and love our neighbor as we love ourselves*. If we don't care enough about our own life to lovingly care for our own well-being, how can we contribute to anyone else's well-being? We can only love someone else to the extent we have learned to love ourselves. And until we understand God's great love for us by seeking Him daily for a closer relationship through prayer and studying His written Word, the Holy Bible, we will continue to be severely handicapped in our ability to love God, ourselves, and others.

And by self-love, I am not referring to self-esteem. To love ourselves means making healthy choices for our well-being. To esteem ourselves means thinking highly of ourselves, which implies we think lowlier of others. Healthy self-love overflows into good deeds through a heart filled with the knowledge of God's love for us that compels us to share that love with others. Self-esteem, on the other hand, keeps its focus on doing whatever will build pride in ourselves and enhance our self-image. There is a huge difference between self-love and self-esteem.

IGNORING THE SOURCE OF POWER

It is a sad reality the average Christian rarely or never reads their Bible. Therefore, the average Christian lives by distorted views of Christianity passed on from other unstudied, immature Christians or the worldly wisdom that rides the airwaves daily and is propagated through the surrounding unbelieving carnal world that is focused on pleasure and self-interest. That being the case, the average Christian is dominated by a fear-based or self-concerned decision-based system because that is what worldly sources promote. The world-based, or, we could say, Satan-based, system seeks to influence the decisions of the masses through fear or temptation to immediately gratify our five carnal senses of taste, touch, smell, hearing, and sight. Even pastors and other church leaders are not immune to these enemy tactics.

Satan has effectively stolen, killed, and destroyed the abundant life of many Christians by infiltrating the body of Christ with false teachings over centuries by distorting the truth into half-truths and telling outright lies that align with worldly system thinking and practices. So, here again, we come back to our need to **know God intimately** so we can decipher which of the tens of thousands of thoughts that go through our minds daily are from God and which are from the Enemy of our souls.

RECOGNIZING TRUTH

God once told the prophet Jeremiah to influence the people instead of letting unbelieving people influence him. I am saddened to see that in many Christian churches today, the worldly system of beliefs seems to be affecting them more than the truths of God recorded in the Bible.

I want to add a personal disclaimer here, however. Having lived seventy-one years, and having been proven wrong at times when I was a hundred percent sure I was right, I am not singling out or casting stones at anyone or any church body or denomination. I am still in my own learning and perfecting process and am constantly seeking God for wisdom and truth so I am not misled in my own biases developed over a lifetime. That is why I am constantly self-analyzing my thoughts, words, and actions against God's character that He is perfecting me into. I know the abundant life for each of us lies on the path God has planned for us as individuals, and I do not want to stray from my path because that is where peace, joy, and overflowing blessings are located. My path would not be a blessing to you because it was designed for me. Your path would not be a blessing for me because it has been designed for you. That is why we individually must seek God our Father for our path.

Truth is found in God and His Words. Anything we believe that does not align with God's words recorded in the Bible must be questioned. In fact, I question everything because I want to be fully aligned with God's will for my life and recognize His Truth. God's Word is spiritually discerned, so we must rely on that inner witness of the Holy Spirit and the counsel of mature believers who have consistently demonstrated the unconditional love of Jesus if we want to experience the ultimate abundant life Christ's blood purchased for us. We cannot fully rely on any human being for truth.

Chapter 3:

LIVING THE GRACE-FILLED LIFE

Finishing Well

I have come to question if any of us have ever really had an original thought. I wonder whether every thought going through our minds is either from God or Satan. Partially, I ponder the question because every human being that has ever lived, or will ever live, is a unique creation of God, with unique talents, abilities, interests, desires, and unique contribution to this race of humanity and to stewarding the earth and everything in it. Therefore, our thoughts are directing us individually each day in our choices. Someone is directing us in a particular direction; we simply decide which voices to listen to. God's voice leads us down a path of peace, abundance, overflowing blessings, and healthy, life-giving outcomes. Satan's voice leads us down a path where we encounter anxiety, fear, lack, poverty, resentment, bitterness—the list of negatives is nearly endless.

Contrary to the world's message that *we can be anything we want to be*, we are individually designed for a specific purpose or purposes, with unique talents, abilities, and desires. Inner peace and contentment comes only when we accept our designed purpose as directed by the voice of the Holy Spirit. And, as I have said many times, *there are no unimportant jobs.* Our world and our lives only work optimally when we each put one hundred percent effort into being everything God created us as individuals to be. It is the worldly system leaders in various arenas that attempt to mold us into servants to achieve their desired outcomes.

To experience the abundant life that Christ's sacrifice purchased for us, we must be sensitive to the Spirit of Truth's voice guiding our path. We have a real enemy, who is interested only in destroying us. That is why we must develop our sensitivity to God's Spirit of Truth.

John 10:10-11
"The thief's purpose is to steal and kill and destroy. My purpose is to give them a rich and satisfying life. I am the good shepherd. The good shepherd sacrifices his life for the sheep."

Proverbs 3:5-6
"Trust in the LORD with all your heart; do not depend on your own understanding. Seek his will in all you do, and he will show you which path to take."

So, my question to you is, *who are you listening to?* If you live in fear, anxiety, and worry, you are listening to the wrong voices. If you live confidently with inner peace, regardless of circumstances, you are anchored in the truth of God's love and faithfulness and hearing His guidance.

SOURCE OF SENSITIVITY

To realize inner confidence and peace, we must grow in intimacy and sensitivity to the voice of the Holy Spirit—so how do we do that? Let's turn to a couple directions from Jesus.

John 5:24
"I tell you the truth, those who listen to my message and believe in God who sent me have eternal life. They will never be condemned for their sins, but they have already passed from death into life."

John 6:63
"The Spirit alone gives eternal life. Human effort accomplishes nothing. And the very words I have spoken to you are spirit and life."

God's words, revealed to us through the indwelling Spirit of Truth, are spirit and life to us. To become more in-tune with the voice of the Holy Spirit within us, as believers, it is imperative that we saturate our minds with God's written word in the Holy Bible. As we do, the Holy Spirit fine-tunes our spiritual ears to His voice and causes us to recognize truthful thoughts from God versus worldly thoughts from the Enemy of our souls.

If we get all our direction and concepts for our life via worldly sources that are purposely designed to keep us controlled through anger and fear or entice us to spend money on products or temporary pleasures to accommodate the selfish desires of the influencers, how can we expect to experience God's peace? Peace and wisdom come through prayer and saturating our heart and soul (defined as mind, will, emotions) with the knowledge of God's love and desires for us.

As we continually seek God through daily Bible study, our heart and mind become increasingly sensitized over time to the Holy Spirit's voice so we more clearly recognize it as opposed to the voice of the world and those who come to steal our peace, joy, contentment, faith, and blessings reserved for us by God.

KNOWING YOURSELF

"The two most important days in your life are the day you are born and the day you find out why." – Mark Twain.

Doubtless, the most important question you require an accurate answer to is: *"Who am I, and what was I born to be and do?"* Are you living your life according to God-given desires and dreams or according to the direction and guidance of other influential people in your life? Your influencers take many identities: parents, siblings, relatives, coaches, teachers, friends, neighbors, advertisers, pastors and priests, world cultures, news outlets, and a multitude of others. So, are you living God's design for you, or have you been conformed into the combined image of a multitude of other influencers? Perpetual inner-peace and fulfillment will never be a reality for you until you are living the life God created you to live.

I believe one litmus test to determine if you are on the right path lies in the state of your heart and soul. Are you living with an inner-peace of heart that allows you to make healthy and rational decisions for yourself and others, or are you living with constant anxiety and feeling pressure to perform in a certain way or to help others achieve their desires while abandoning your own?

Due to the way God has pre-wired me, I not only feel, understand, empathize with, and show mercy to others who struggle, I also feel my own pain more intensely. By far, emotional pains throughout my life have been far more devastating than any physical pain. I was setup for emotional pain through words of others when I was a youth and younger man that caused me to feel like I didn't matter. And as everyone has, I experienced multiple rejections of various types that left me with a self-image that said I was less-than compared to others who were more educated, popular, or successful according to worldly standards. It has taken me many years to recognize I believed lies about me that caused me to unconsciously doubt God's love for me. I was longing for God's love and acceptance by seeking my validation through others. If they rejected me, in my mind, God was rejecting me too. I was not *fully* convinced of God's love for me. God has had to take me the long way around the proverbial barn to prove His love and faithfulness toward me. He has faithfully, tenderly, and persistently found ways to prove His love for me and clearly reveal to me His active perfecting process in my life as He leads me through life, connecting all my dots since before birth—always protecting, always providing. One of the most precious words God spoke to my heart years ago was, "*Yes. You are flawed like everyone else, but I love you anyway.*" God loves you too. Being fully persuaded of that fact leads to enjoying the abundant life designed for you.

Having finally come to this KNOWING God's love for me has set me free from the fears of rejection by others. Knowing in my heart God is pleased with me and has nothing but love and goodness to share with me has set me free to enjoy life as me. It is this *knowing* that sets us free to pursue our God-given path, free from the misguided influence of others and from the many various spirits of fear.

FATEFUL REQUESTS

When I was around five years old, I remember sitting in church watching a baptism. As I sat there, I asked God in my heart to make me a pastor so I could help others know about Jesus. Even at that age, I loved Jesus and felt close to Him. I never became an ordained pastor, but I have served in ministry through a variety of leadership capacities for over forty years. I do not believe any of that service has been of my own doing or by accident or happenstance. I believe every opportunity to serve has somehow been directly orchestrated by God to fulfill the request of that young boy.

The second request, and confession, intimately connects with the first. It was a beautiful sunny June day when I was a young teenager. I remember looking up to heaven, raising my hands and saying, *"God, I don't have a clue what to do with my life, so you are going to have to take me by the hand and lead me through life, take me where I should go, and show me what I should do."*

I thank God that at such a young age, He gave me the realization I am incapable of planning my own life. Without going into the many details of how God has and continues to fulfill those requests, I confirm to you that God has wonderfully fulfilled those requests. I have no idea how to explain how God works in our lives to accomplish His good will and pleasure, but I know that He has been intimately involved in my life to serve and be served. If you haven't yet, I would encourage you to make that same acknowledgement and request. God is infinitely wiser than we are, and as His children, He wants to be intimately involved in our lives for good. We just need to let go of thinking we have to do it all on our own and ignorantly believing we can formulate a better plan for our lives than God can.

Psalm 32:8
"The LORD says, 'I will guide you along the best pathway for your life. I will advise you and watch over you.'"

Psalm 37:23-24
"The LORD directs the steps of the godly. He delights in every detail of their lives. Though they stumble, they will never fall for the LORD holds them by the hand."

Once in prayer, God spoke to my heart, saying, **"What's important to My children is important to Me."** This is another area many Christians have been deceived in through distorted beliefs. Many in Christian circles seem to believe God is only interested in our working for Him, as though He needs anything, and that He is not concerned with our creature comforts and desires. I can most assuredly testify that God, our perfect Father, is concerned with our complete well-being—body, soul, and spirit! There is not a desire of my heart that God, my Father, has not fulfilled over time. In fact, He has blessed me far beyond anything I ever expected to enjoy in this life as I have faithfully sought to live a life pleasing to Him and sought Him daily for increasing truth, wisdom, and closeness. It also testifies to Jesus's admonition that if we seek the kingdom of God first and foremost, all those things the unbelieving world daily seeks after will be added to us as rewards for placing our highest priority on seeking a relationship with Him and pointing others to Jesus.

EMBRACING YOUR CALLING

God created us from water and dirt and then breathed His life into us. Eventually, these earthly vessels will quit flowing life-giving blood, become dormant, evaporate, and dissolve back into the earthly elements from whence we came. The big question that most, if not all of us, struggle with is what to do with and through these earthly vessels while we are living here on this beautiful planet the LORD created specifically for our well-being.

In a real sense, we are called by God to live out our *God-designed program* with one-hundred percent effort and *enjoy each day of it*. King Solomon, as recorded in the Book Ecclesiastes, recognized our work in this earthly life to be a blessing from God. Enjoying our work is, in fact, one of our greatest blessings when we learn to accept the work God has assigned each of us. Everything we accomplish pales in comparison to the joy involved in the work-process of actually bringing our work to successful completion in service to our families, all of humanity, and all of Earth's creation.

I am daily awestruck by the complexity of the world, the earth, and everything in it and how somehow, with all our different likes, dislikes, opinions, internal and external struggles, and battles with evil in the world, God keeps everything connected and flowing relatively smoothly. Every person on Earth has a specific role to fulfill in providing for the well-being of all life on Earth. I cannot overemphasize the need to joyfully embrace your life's calling if you want to enjoy life and finish well, with joy and peace and contentment in your heart.

If you are in law enforcement, I thank you for keeping society safe and putting your life on the line daily. If you are in the military, I thank you for keeping this country and its citizens safe on a daily basis. I have served in both, and I remember feeling a sense of privilege and responsibility putting my life on the line for my family, community, and country. I hope you feel the same privilege. If you are involved in education, I thank you and pray you take your responsibility seriously to help each child realize his or her God-given calling and potential. Teaching is a tremendous responsibility and privilege. If you are in a service industry, making hotel rooms ready for guests, waiting tables in a restaurant, performing janitorial services, or any number of other service-related occupations, I want to emphasize that you are invaluable. It takes every individual performing their job with excellence to keep our earthly lives functioning well.

We are all called to perform our work as doing it unto the LORD, and I do believe that if we do that, God will find ways to compensate us for our devotion to, in essence, loving unconditionally through serving with a good attitude. I also know that monetary wages are not the root source of our joy and contentment. I have encountered miserable wealthy people and happy, content persons living on the street with no material wealth. Our joy comes from within and is a gift from God through the work of the Holy Spirit.

SEPARATING BEHAVIOR FROM THE OFFENDER

I believe one of our most difficult challenges is separating the person from the action. How do you hate evil actions without hating the person who did them? Carried to one extreme are those in society today who refuse to punish anyone for their actions, instead making excuses for their behaviors based on the person's upbringing or life circumstances. At the other extreme are those showing no compassion and wanting to lock up and throw away the key for all offenders, believing we can live in peace if we just get rid of all those *bad people*. We know this obviously won't work because God spent thousands of years proving we are incapable of perfect behavior. So, we obviously have an obligation to deal with both—the behavior and the person's soul and spirit.

I would even suggest the person we resist showing mercy and compassion to could be ourselves. We, more than anyone, know when we blow it. Without embracing our forgiveness, we can fall prey to punishing ourselves repeatedly for a single thoughtless moment. This is not God's will for us. Once a sin is recognized and confessed, we should refuse to think on it anymore. I would recommend reviewing chapter 10 in the Book of Hebrews at this point to realize the freedom Christ purchased—the freedom to live a guilt-free life. *If God doesn't remember our sins as redeemed children, why do we allow Satan to continually condemn us? Remember, he is the Father of Lies.*

GRACE VERSUS LAW

The Bible clearly identifies the law to be for the lawless ones in society. To maintain peace and orderliness, law and punishment is necessary. For the Christian who has surrendered their heart to Christ Jesus, the law isn't necessary because the *desire of every born-again believer is to be right and do right*. We are self-correcting in essence, and the Holy Spirit of God within us convicts us of wrong actions and prompts us to repent and correct our choices in those particular areas as we keep moving forward. However, there is another purpose, as the apostle Paul pointed out: The Law reveals to us our imperfection and need for Christ's redeeming sacrifice. The Law—the Ten Commandments—has not lost its purpose.

Your *Finishing Well* path may be filled with challenges, but seeking God daily for increased wisdom and revelation of His love for you leads to increasing inner-peace and contentment as God continues perfecting you into His image. Your receiving is still contingent upon embracing your unique design and calling, however, which only God can show you. You cannot receive your purpose and life direction from anyone other than God because you are a unique creation. And since we all have a bias toward our own uniqueness, we can unknowingly influence others to adapt their life's direction to our calling and understanding if we aren't careful to avoid that inclination. We are no one's god, so we are simply called to point others to Jesus and the Bible to receive their individual direction from God.

THE GREATNESS OF GOD

I am daily awestruck with how God has created us with unique gifting to serve each other for well-being. I think of the millions of people around the world working at this very moment on my behalf and yours to produce and provide food and products for our sustenance and enjoyment and well-being. It is impossible to fully grasp the vastness of what it takes to get everything we need to us daily; often while we take these things for granted. I do not! We have become a very self-centered and entitlement-minded world for the most part, with very little appreciation or gratitude for basically having everything we need at our fingertips. To overcome our entitlement- inclination requires a renewed focus on God's goodness and mercy that provides for our every need and desire. And, inner peace comes with a focus on His great faithfulness. Forgive us, LORD!

INEVITABLE FAITH TESTS

Whenever you take a stand for your convictions, as defined by God versus accepting the world's distorted belief system, you will find your faith tested. Many times, faith-challenges will come from within your own family and close acquaintances. Your faith in God's promises (detailed in the Bible) is also tested when you feel symptoms of illness coming against your body, face challenging life decisions, job insecurity attempts to make you anxious, when your children seem to be heading in an unhealthy direction, and in a multitude of other ways throughout life.

While writing this book, I experienced mental and emotional skirmishes that I hadn't encountered in years, and I have fought back symptoms of illness through God's promise to turn sickness away from me as a believer who lives in His Presence. And, per God's promises, Christ's Spirit within me has enabled me to successfully stand against those enemy attacks by rebuking them in the name of Jesus through undoubting faith. As I discussed earlier, it is primarily doubt and unbelief that prevents God's working in our lives. We must be *fully persuaded* as our father in the faith, Abraham, confidently believed that *God's promises are faithful and true* (Phil. 4:13).

Our Enemy has already been defeated, but he has a loud voice and uses it to discourage Christians and deceive us out of our confident walk of faith and the blessings available to us through confident, non-doubting faith. Therefore, again, it is imperative that we saturate our heart and soul with God's promises and words through daily seeking wisdom, understanding, and knowledge through prayer, reading our Bible, and fellowshipping with mature Christians who can assist us in our walk of faith until we become fully convinced in our heart and soul that *all things are possible for God and for those who believe.*

The road to the end of our earthly life does involve trials and temptations, but we have the Spirit of the Living God inside us to strengthen, comfort, instruct, and guide us along our path so we can maintain our gift of inner-peace that Christ freely gives.

WHAT MAKES PURSUITS RIGHT OR WRONG – GODLY OR UNGODLY?

Answers to that question vary widely among Christians and non-Christians alike. The world promotes self-fulfilling goals and seeking self-fulfillment. Many in Christian circles claim that seeking any worldly-realized fulfillment is ungodly. So, what is God's will concerning our desires? Are all desires met through worldly resources wrong? First, it all depends on what you define as worldly. Some think any pleasures in the world are ungodly, so they live lives of self-righteous dissatisfaction. We must realize that "worldly" is a system of operation that incorporates beliefs and customs that fight against God's will. So, I would argue that it all depends on our motives. God says that He looks at the heart to see our true intents and purposes in every choice we make.

God created our bodies from earthly elements, and we continue to need earthly resources to sustain our lives and provide for every physical need. God, in many Scripture verses, says He takes pleasure in prospering those who seek Him, trust Him, and acknowledge Him as Lord and Savior of their lives. Having wealth and physical resources is not sin unless covetousness is the motive and driving force. It is *the love of money* that is the source of all evil—not money. We live in a world that runs on money, and we need it for every resource to sustain our lives and provide temporary protection and enjoyment as we live out this earthly existence. We also need it to finance spreading the Good News.

Some questions might be helpful in evaluating this dilemma. Would God give you desires for things or ambitions that He has no plans to use for your well-being or to fulfill His overall purposes for humanity? Would the God of all power, wisdom, and sufficiency and Creator of all things not want to share those with grateful and thankful children? Why would God have *given* Abraham, Jacob, David, Solomon, and others great wealth if He was opposed to His faithful servants and children enjoying earthly joys and resources? No, God is *not* against wealth or any other healthy enjoyment in this earthly life.

Proverbs 10:22
"The blessing of the LORD makes a person rich, and he adds no sorrow with it."

Where does ungodliness come into the equation? It is through *perversion*. When we take the good gifts and resources God has given us for sustenance and enjoyment and pervert their use, we cross the line. When we rebel against God's design for our lives as individuals and against God's design for humanity, we harvest the results of physical illness, broken relationships, poverty, sexually-transmitted diseases, wars, physical, emotional, and mental abuse, anxiety, dissatisfaction with life – the list goes on and on.

But when our entire being focuses on growing in the knowledge of God's love for us and the rest of humanity, we enter into that godly rest for our souls and hearts that prompt us to serve humanity from the overflow of love that develops in our heart. If we are earnestly pursuing closeness with God, peace of heart and soul should be the norm—not the exception.

As I said earlier, we are all created with unique desires and gifts. I would suggest *finishing well* is achieved by embracing the life God created for us as unique individuals to live. This is where the complications come in. From my experience, I suspect few people have fully embraced their designed life. Most are living the life they feel forced upon them or a life they have been influenced by other sources to pursue and live.

DAILY LIFE CHOICES

There is a saying I have heard through many varied sources, and it is absolutely true: *We all serve either God or Satan.* Those are the only two choices. But how do we know which we are serving, especially if we are Christian but still struggle with the question? The answer is usually evidenced by our life choices. If we have embraced our God-given design and are flowing in it, we will likely be experiencing continuous inner-peace and contentment.

Your design may lead to much effort and work, but you will experience a peace of heart that those of the world cannot understand as you go about serving humanity and creation per your design. If you are constantly filled with anxiety, confusion, mental and emotional anguish, and even continual battles with physical illnesses, I would suggest you prayerfully seek God, and perhaps professional Christian counseling, to understand the source of the spiritual battle. *Behind the battle is a spirit of fear in some form* fighting to keep you from enjoying the path God intends for you.

UNGOLDY INFLUENCERS

This may sound strange to many Christian believers, but well-meaning Christians many times are the greatest source of misdirection in our lives. Through distorted teachings and doctrines that pressure born-again believers to continue living under the Old Covenant of trying to appease God through perfect performance, we can cave in to the influence of powerful personalities who promote a direction of life based on their limited understanding to drive us to try being an eagle when we are created a lion.

Ironically, to me, many times the tolerance and acceptance of unbelievers in society mimics the love of God more than we see in many self-righteous, legalistic Christian churches. There is a line which can't be crossed, however, and this is it. Christ Jesus has called us to live out unconditional love toward all people, but that does not mean condoning perverted and unhealthy behaviors. Unconditional love is compassionate, loving, and gentle toward others, but it does not say right is wrong and wrong is right to appease those desiring to live ungodly (unhealthy) lives. Tolerance and acceptance of behaviors condemned in the Bible have crept into many churches today, as no Christian wants to be considered unkind or intolerant. Unkindness goes against the very nature of God. So, how do we deal with this?

God's laws, rules, and precepts are all centered on a singular purpose: giving us a guideline to experiencing life and blessings and harmony between God and man and between man and man. God is all about love, compassion, and generosity. Satan has twisted God's perfect will to convince us God is a punitive creator waiting to punish every unhealthy choice. Satan has kept much of the body of Christ still anxiously trying to appease a Holy God through a performance-based rating system that has never worked. Humanity seems to love having a set of rules to judge rightness or wrongness. That is not how God operates. Yes, God will forever reject those who reject Him, but for those of us who have acknowledged Him as LORD and received His in-dwelling Holy Spirit, we have been forever cleansed and made righteous through the Blood of Jesus. Any good works we do should be from overflowing hearts of love—not to earn points with God or from fearing punishment.

LET PEACE RULE IN YOUR HEART

<u>John 14:27</u>
"I am leaving you with a gift – peace of mind and heart. And the peace I give is a gift the world cannot give. So don't be troubled or afraid."

<u>Colossians 3:12-15</u>
"Since God chose you to be the holy people he loves, you must clothe yourselves with tenderhearted mercy, kindness, humility, gentleness, and patience. **Make allowance for each other's faults, and forgive anyone who offends you.** *Remember, the Lord forgave you, so you must forgive others. Above all, clothe yourselves with love, which binds us all together in perfect harmony.* **And let the peace that comes from Christ rule in your hearts.** *For as*

members of one body you are called to live in peace. **And always be thankful.**"

If we allow our self-concern, self-will, and the spirit of fear to dictate the thoughts of our life, it will interfere with the gift of peace of heart and mind that Christ freely offers believers. It is possible to live a fearless and care-free life, but it is maintained through an inner-anchored knowledge of God's love for us as demonstrated through Christ Jesus, willingly exchanging His life for ours. He died to provide us with a life of abundance—abundance of inner peace, external protection, and abundant provision of resources—both for our own well-being and enjoyment and to freely share that goodness with others.

God is a generous and compassionate Giver, and every believer has been given a new heart that desires to be a generous giver as well. The *Spirit of Fear*, evidenced through symptoms of greed, anger, envy, jealousy, self-righteousness, stinginess, oppression, cruelty, resentment, and so on, comes from Satan, who only comes to steal, kill, and destroy our spirit, soul, and body. Contrary to the Spirit of Fear's mission, ***God's spirit of love is given to produce a satisfying life and produce in and through us the fruit of God's Spirit.***

Galatians 5:22
"*But the Holy Spirit produces this kind of fruit in our lives: love, joy, peace, patience, kindness, goodness, faithfulness, gentleness, and self-control. There is no law against these things!*"

BELIEVE – FORGIVE – SPEAK – RECEIVE

Jesus presented a formula, per se, for receiving answered prayer.

Mark 11:22-26 (emphasis added)
"Then Jesus said to the disciples, 'Have faith in God. I tell you the truth, you can say to this mountain, 'May you be lifted up and thrown into the sea,' and it will happen. But have no doubt in your heart. ***I tell you, you can pray for anything, and if you believe that you've received it, it will be yours. But when you are praying, first forgive*** *anyone you are holding a grudge against, so that your Father in heaven will forgive your sins, too.'"*

There are several truths in those words. First, Jesus said to have faith in God. If we approach God without expectation or faith in His ability and character to care for us, we are essentially in unbelief, and according to Apostle James, we can expect nothing from God. Faith, as evidenced in the many miracles of healing Jesus did, opens us to receiving our prayer's manifested fulfillment.

When we pray in faith, Jesus instructed us to believe we have *already received* what we pray for, and we *will receive it*. What's He saying? If we pray and don't see it immediately manifested physically, how can we already have received it? I would suggest it means that God has already answered the prayer and what we prayed for is on the way, either by speedy delivery or the slow boat *to arrive at God's appointed time.*

Secondly, however, forgiveness is integrally tied to receiving. If we hold resentment and bitterness in our hearts, we will not be praying from pure hearts and motives. If praying with un-forgiveness in our hearts, we have hearts with open doors to the Devil. That being the case, we will not be praying the perfect will of God because our hearts will have been polluted and cannot be praying in harmony with God's will from pure heart intentions.

Thirdly, when praying with fully-persuaded conviction, having examined our hearts and confessed any unforgiveness to free ourselves from the Devil's hold and spoken our request aligning with God's revealed will, *we will receive our request according to Jesus.*

WORK REQUIRED ON OUR PART

John 6:28-29
"They replied, 'We want to perform God's works too. What should we do?' Jesus told them, 'This is the only work God wants from you: Believe in the one he has sent.'"

It saddens me to see so many professed Christians still fearful of upsetting God by making a mistake; so many are still attempting to earn God's favor through their performance. It is most certainly true that works are a critical part of our Christian walk, but again, it comes down to motives. Is our heart so full of the knowledge of God's love for us that it overflows with good works out of a grateful and thankful heart? Or are the works generated out of a sense of *owing* God for Christ's sacrifice on the cross that compels us to spend our life paying Him back? From my experience, I think the second scenario is most prevalent, but it isn't always obvious.

If your scenario is the first, then you will understand His love for you caused Him to freely give His life in exchange for yours. That is a gift you cannot repay. If you could repay it, it would not be a gift—it would be a bargain between you and God, as the second scenario reflects. This perspective sets you free to enjoy life and freely overflow God's love to others as the Holy Spirit moves you.

The second scenario compels you to feel you must pay God back for His sacrifice. If you adopt the notion you must earn salvation, you will spend your life always knowing in your heart you are coming up short because you cannot possibly, through your own effort, pay back the price of salvation. I personally think this is one of the great lies Satan has woven into the fabric of much of the body of Christ, thereby stealing the joy and freedom Christ purchased for us.

So, let's simply believe, receive His love and Holy Spirit, then allow that love to freely flow through us to the world around us without thought of earning God's pleasure through our works. To be free, we must focus on God's goodness rather than our ill-fated works-attempts to please God. Perhaps a verse from Hebrews will help this explanation.

Hebrews 11:6
"And it is impossible to please God without faith. Anyone who wants to come to him must believe that God exists and that he rewards those who sincerely seek him."

The truth that God rewards us simply for believing in Him and seeking to grow intimacy daily with Him seems to be lost on too many Christians. God rewards us with *every good thing* as we simply seek Him. When I say *seek Him*, I refer to seeking Him for understanding concerning His love for us, first and foremost, because if we don't understand His love for us and acceptance of us, we will have little godly love to share. Without that proper perspective, our default will be to love based on performance, as the world of unbelievers does.

LOVE AND FREEDOM

It is the heart-realized love of God that sets us free to be ourselves and resist pressure from the world and others in our lives to mold us into their image, and their distorted imagined image for our lives. As long as we live in fear of what others think of us, fear of disappointing others' expectations for us, or acting in ways that leave us feeling empty inside to please others for fear of them rejecting us, we will forfeit the freedom in Christ to enjoy life abundantly.

You will never be whole—body, soul, and spirit—until you intimately know God as your Best Friend, Who will never judge you, reject you, condemn you for poor choices, or try to mold you into anything other than the perfect unique self He created you to be. You will never be happy or content trying to be what others say you should be. You find your fulfillment in being the unique individual God created you to be. And, God is perfectly willing, able, and seeking to guide your heart daily down the path prepared specifically for you. I am fully convinced that your inner-peace will be maintained as you follow His inner-guidance daily and resist outside pressure to conform to any other image.

Jesus died to make you *perfect* in His sight. *When you really believe you have already been made perfect in God's sight through Christ, as clearly revealed in Hebrews, chapter 10,* as well as elsewhere, you will realize the freedom you have to live free of all fear-demons.

THE SPIRIT THAT OVERCOMES FEAR

Until you truly understand and deal with the source of fear and anger, you will continue to be captive to these enemies of your mind and emotions—or, at least, be constantly influenced by them.

<u>2 Timothy 1:7</u>
"For God has not given us a spirit of fear and timidity, but of power, love, and self-discipline."

<u>2 Timothy 1:7 (KJV)</u>
"For God hath not given us the spirit of fear; but of power, and of love, and of a sound mind."

We are told repeatedly throughout Scripture not to fear because there is torment in fear, and God does not seek to torment any of His children—the body of Christ. Fear is always rooted in self-concern. Jealousy is the manifested fear of losing something precious to us. Anger is fear of not having things go our way or the way we think they should. The spirit of envy is fear of missing out on the good things we see others possess. Every negative human emotion in one way or another is rooted in our being deceived by *the spirit of fear*. This is immensely important to understand because our battles are initiated in the spiritual realm. It is probably helpful to understand that the spirit of fear intimately connects to our prideful fallen-nature. When we rely on our own abilities to successfully live life, we are doomed to experience the negative mental, emotional, and physical symptoms generated by the spirit of fear. Our freedom from fear is only found in fully persuaded confidence in God's Spirit to protect and provide.

God has provided us five physical senses to fully enjoy this physical life He has provided us on Earth, but our physical senses, left uncontrolled, lead us into all sorts of trouble and poor choices. A modern psychological phenomenon is labeled FOMO, or "Fear Of Missing Out." Actually, FOMO had its origins in the Garden of Eden when Satan convinced Eve that God was holding out on them. In her *fear of missing out*, Eve caved to deception and temptation, and Adam willingly followed. Today, our soul is still stuck in between our spirit and our five senses. The condition of our soul (mind, will, emotions) determines our moment-by-moment choices throughout life. It isn't difficult to see the state of a person's soul by observing their life choices. The question we face is: *Will we allow our five senses to dictate our soul's decision-making process, or will we listen to the perfect will of God through the Holy Spirit's inner guiding voice to make healthy choices?*

WALKING IN TRUTH: GOD'S REQUIREMENTS

John 6:28-29
"They replied, 'We want to perform God's works too. What should we do?' Jesus told them, 'This is the only work God wants from you: Believe in the one he has sent.'"

Micah 6:8
"No, O people, the LORD has told you what is good, and this is what he requires of you: to do what is right, to love mercy, and to walk humbly with your God."

John 13:34-35 (emphasis added)
*"So now I am giving you a new commandment: **Love each other**. Just as I have loved you, you should love each other. Your love for one another will prove to the world that you are my disciples."*

Tying those verses together with Hebrews chapter 10 provides a better understanding of how Jesus instructs us to live. First, we walk forever cleansed of our sin through the sacrificial blood of Jesus, as explained in Hebrews chapter 10. Second, through the power and direction of the Holy Spirit, Who lives within us, as believers, we propagate the unconditional love of Jesus to those around us and throughout the world. *Our mission as Christians is to love as God in Christ Jesus evidenced His love toward us.*

John 14:15-18 (emphasis added)
*"**If you love me, obey my commandments**. And I will ask the Father, and he will give you another Advocate, who will never leave you. He is the Holy Spirit, who leads into all truth. The world cannot receive him, because it isn't looking for him and doesn't recognize him. But you know him, because he lives with you now and later will be in you. No, I will not abandon you as orphans. I will come to you."*

In New Testament records, we find Christ Jesus adding to the Church daily, and He did this by the Holy Spirit working through believers. Jesus said many times it was the Father in Him performing miracles; so, in essence, we, as believers, live with the constant presence of God in us. Therefore, all power, all wisdom, all knowledge, all understanding, and unconditional love lives within every believer. The key to releasing that power and experiencing all the Holy Spirit has to offer us is faith and shedding all unbelief. It is doubt, unforgiveness, and unbelief that most often limit God's work in and through us. But unleashing the power of the Holy Spirit within us starts with knowledge—knowledge of God's truth—and truth comes to us through God's Word—the Holy Bible.

I cannot overemphasis enough the need to saturate your heart and soul with God's recorded testimony, the Holy Bible, if you want to live a victorious life filled with inner peace and rest for your soul. In addition, attending church, integrating into Bible Study groups, hearing biblically-based preaching, and fellowshipping with mature Christians all contribute to the wellness of your spirit, soul, and body. But I have experienced too many distorted personal opinions passed on through some preaching and church leaders to put my complete trust in them for truth. **The Bible is the only source from which complete truth emanates.** I encourage you to question everything you hear or see and test it against God's character and directions as revealed in the Bible.

SUFFERINGS OF THE FAITHFUL

There are some unanswerable questions when it comes to believers experiencing suffering, but many times, the reason for suffering is obvious because there is a direct cause-effect relationship. Some obvious examples are getting lung cancer from smoking, dying from liver disease through alcoholism, contracting various health issues due to obesity caused by overeating unhealthy diets, sexually transmitted diseases from illicit sexual behaviors, and etcetera.

But what about the faithful Christian who has consistently made healthy choices throughout life according to God's will and character, but still ends up with cancer or other terminal illness? These are cases where we may never get a satisfactory answer. But, I have witnessed too many miracle healings resulting from prayers of faith to question God's reality and presence. I have to believe in these cases where prayers seem to go unanswered that the person's suffering is not in vain; God will work good out of it somehow for someone.

<u>Romans 8:28</u>
"And we know that God causes everything to work together for the good of those who love God and are called according to his purpose for them."

So, this is one of those situations where I encourage you to maintain your faith and find reasons for thanksgiving and gratitude when healing is not manifested through your prayers. You can be assured you or your loved one in Christ is not suffering in vain. God does not waste pain. Painful situations are accomplishing some good, even if we never come to understand it. But, if uncalled for suffering comes your way, pray and maintain your faith because prayer combined with faith is a powerful healing combination. If you doubt that, see in the gospels how many times Jesus told the healed person their faith had made them well or whole. The fact is also recorded that unbelief limited the ability of Jesus to heal, so undoubting faith accomplishes much. I hate to leave it there because we all like definitive answers as to why things happen. Unfortunately, we are not always given the answer, so our faith gets tested and refined.

There is another suffering of the faithful that needs addressing, however. Our flesh (sight, smell, taste, hearing, touch) are powerful forces, and they constantly work on our soul (mind, will, emotions) for appeasement. The flesh wants what the flesh wants, and these senses, as I addressed earlier, have been given to us by God to fully enjoy this earthly life and warn us of danger. Those who have acknowledged Christ as LORD and Savior have received a *new heart* from God, and that new, pure heart wants what the heart wants. So, we have this constant battle going on in our soul's decision-making process—listen to the new, pure spirit-heart or cave to the cravings of the flesh. In a very real sense, our thoughts, words, and choices reveal the level of maturity in Christ our souls have achieved.

THE ONE JOYFUL SUFFERING

There is one type of suffering we are unanimously called to experience with pure joy—suffering rejection, ridicule, and perhaps, life-surrendering suffering for spreading the Good News or simply being a Christ-follower. I have experienced this joy personally. When I have been persecuted for simply being a Christ-follower, I remember doing it with peace in my heart. There was an unexplainable joy simply from knowing my faith was evident to the unbelieving world. I pray that your faith is also evident to the unbelieving world as a testimony to them and, perhaps, against them. I also pray your maturing faith is an example to strengthen other believers in their faith-maturation process.

CALLED INTO THE BATTLE

We are called to stand against evil through the authority given to us in the name of Jesus. We overcome evil with love; love for self or anyone else involves effort. The godly will not prevail entirely by passively praying God will fix everything. Our prayers effect change, but God works primarily through people to accomplish His purposes, so we, as believers, must be sensitive to the Holy Spirit's nudge and guidance as to our individual involvement in that process.

I would say natural disasters are the one exception. The words recorded in the Holy Bible clearly show God is Sovereign and can, and does at times, control the weather and the entire universe to accomplish His purposes. And I have personally experienced God controlling the weather through prayer in specific instances. My personal belief is God will allow natural disasters to get our attention if we continue in a rebellious state. Natural disasters are acts in nature that we have no control over. These devastating disasters drive many people to seek God through prayer, and they drive masses to demonstrate godly love through self-sacrificial service to help those in need, causing the recipients to thank and glorify God.

WORLD AT WAR: NEED FOR GODLY WISDOM

In the context of war we see the great paradox of humanity revealed. We see the evil in those raping, pillaging, ripping open the bellies of pregnant women, and killing for pleasure. And we see the good in those who sacrifice their lives to rescue the wounded and helpless without regard for their own lives. War clearly reveals the worst and best in humanity: Satan ruling through those devoted to evil, and God ruling through His redeemed.

However, the paradox is revealed in the inconsistencies. At times, the same person operates on both sides of that fence, depending on particular situations and circumstances. Consistency in selfless service comes from a firm and intimate connection to God. Worldly wisdom will always be situationally dependent, based on the perceived advantage of the individual in their decision-making process. It is only those mature in their faith-connection who will make the right choice, no matter the perceived advantage or disadvantage to them.

BOTTOM LINE

I am convinced most mental, emotional, and physical ailments result from unhealthy stress resulting from a lack of understanding of God's love for us, resulting in a lack of confidence to walk our individual God-ordained path. From birth, we are bombarded with messages from thousands of influences telling us who we should be and what we should want and what we should do. The only One who truly knows our designed purpose and character is God. Until we accept ourselves for who God created us to be and walk through life directed by the Holy Spirit's voice, we will struggle through many fears generated through worldly sources. As I related earlier, however, it all begins with saturating our hearts and souls with God's Testimony—the Holy Scriptures in the Bible—to educate us in God's character and desire for our lives. Living life God's way is the only sensible way to live if we want to experience goodness, favor, and abundance of every good and perfect gift.

We know that *fear is a demonic spirit*. Being fully persuaded of our position in Christ and His love for us frees our soul from the spirit of fear's influence over us. From that confident position, we are able to actively resist voices of fear and discouragement when we hear them. *We can take every thought captive in obedience to Christ* (2 Cor. 10:5). We can perpetually walk with inner-peace. If not, that would make Jesus a liar.

I pray your life is filled with inner-peace overflowing, with every good thing that results in overflowing love and joy to those around you. That is truly God's will for you.

FINAL THOUGHTS

I encourage you to read your Bible with expectation. Expect God to speak to you through it, and continue to increase your knowledge of His great love for you. Christ Jesus clearly stated He was sacrificing His life to provide abundant life for you now and forevermore.

Unbelief and distorted religious beliefs and traditions are still preventing many believers from receiving from God. Work at eliminating any limited expectations you may have adopted through religious traditions of man that place limitations on what God will do and wants to do for you and through you. The God of all creation is certainly a generous God and wants to shower you with blessings. But just as unbelief prevented healing and blessings through Christ Jesus as He walked the earth, unbelief in God's greatness and ignorance of His character and will for your life will limit your life's experience.

Don't let unbelief and limiting expectations keep God's goodness from overflowing abundantly into and through your life. God is a big God, so think and request big. No right desires that God puts in your heart are impossible to fulfill. If God put them there, He will manifest them in His perfect timing.

I leave you with an excerpt from the Book of Colossians:

<u>Colossians 1:19-23a</u>
"For God in all his fullness was pleased to live in Christ, and through him God reconciled everything to himself. He made peace with everything in heaven and on earth by means of Christ's blood on the cross...he has reconciled you to himself through the death of Christ in his physical body. As a result, he has brought you into his own presence, and you are holy and blameless as you stand before him without a single fault. But you must continue to believe this truth and stand firmly in it. Don't drift away from the assurance you received when you heard the Good News."

God will continue to reveal Himself to you as you seek Him for a deeper understanding of His great love for you; and that knowledge will most certainly set you free to be the Real You— the Authentic You.

May God Bless you richly with every good thing reserved for you in Heaven's storehouse.

OTHER BOOKS BY THE AUTHOR

Topic Bible Studies Addressing Everyday Problems and Questions – Series 1
ISBN 1591603986

Topic Bible Studies Addressing Everyday Problems and Questions – Series 2
ISBN 9781615792092

Topic Bible Studies Addressing Everyday Problems and Questions provide thought-provoking, self-searching Bible studies designed to bring you joy, peace, and contentment as you grow to see the Lord Jesus as a faithful and trusted Friend. The study's purpose is to mature your faith to where you can live a stress-free, content life with the inner peace that only God's Holy Spirit can provide.

Seducing Spirits – The Battle for Your Soul
ISBN 978-1-60266-622-1 (hardcopy)
ISBN 978-1-60266-621-4 (paperback)

Most Christians with some level of background in the Scriptures agree that we are involved in spiritual warfare and that in the End Times that battle will intensify. That belief, however, is often a general acknowledgement that Satan is alive and trying to deceive the saints.

Now, in *Seducing Spirits: the Battle for Your Soul,* Dennis Aaberg provides a significant service to the Church by systematically and comprehensively presenting the nature of the spiritual battle we are all called to wage. The various spirits, or demons, that affect a whole range of sinful behavior are identified; the nature of the battle taking place in the heavenly realm is clarified, and the reassuring provision of the Armor of God for our protection is examined. Then, Dennis outlines twenty-seven disciplines that will help you live free in Christ, giving both young and old helpful guidelines that will enable them to resist the seducing spirits of the age.

As with all Minister Aaberg's writings, the entire work is extremely practical, the substance of his thesis is thoroughly biblical, and the abundance of scriptural quotations leaves you with a sense of "Thus saith the Lord!"

Seducing Spirits will sharpen your spiritual perceptions and give you an advantage in victoriously walking with Christ, even in these challenging last days.

Pastor Timothy A. Johnson
Executive Director, Minnesota Church Ministries Association
Bishop/Executive Director, Minnesota Church Ministries Association – Africa

Jesus' Last Seminar – Preaching Love and Unity
ISBN 9781615792436

Knowing His time on Earth was short, Jesus crammed much of Christian theology into a few last words with His disciples in the upper room before His betrayal in the Garden of Gethsemane. Discover the essential teachings of Jesus in *Jesus' Last Seminar,* and then apply them

Other Books by the Author

to your life so you can experience the peace of heart and mind that God wills for you.

Want to be a REAL Man?
ISBN 978-1-62230-455-4

Email: aabergministries@earthlink.net